Ms. Moja Makes Beautiful Clothes

written by
JILL D. DUVALL

photographs by
LILI DUVALL

Reading Consultant
LINDA CORNWELL
Learning Resource Consultant
Indiana Department of Education

CHILDREN'S PRESS® *A Division of Grolier*
New York • London • Hong Kong • Sydney • Danbury, C

Dedicated to H. P.

*Special thanks to Regina, Habia, and Uzikee,
and the staff of Infinite Photo and Imaging*

Library of Congress Cataloging-in-Publication Data
Duvall, Jill.
    Ms. Moja makes beautiful clothes / written by Jill D. Duvall ; photographs by Lili Duvall ; reading consultant, Linda Cornwell.
        p.   cm. — (Our neighborhood)
    Summary: Describes the work done by an African American woman who makes wearable art, all kinds of clothes worn by actors and other performers, and costumes used in museums.
    ISBN 0-516-20314-2 (lib. bdg.)—ISBN 0-516-26151-7 (pbk.)
    1. Costume—Juvenile literature.   2. Sewing—Juvenile literature.
[1. Costume designers. 2. Occupations.] I. Duvall, Lili, ill. II. Title. III. Series: Our neighborhood.
    TT633.D88   1997
    746.9′2—dc20

                              96-34907
                                  CIP
                                  AC

Photographs ©: Lili Duvall

Ms. Januwa Moja is an artist.
But her art does not hang on a wall.
It is art for people to wear!

Ms. Moja designs clothes for actors, dancers, and singers. Her designs are also displayed in museums.

She makes beautiful clothes for people of all shapes and sizes.

Ms. Moja uses African designs in her clothing. Her art shows her community how proud she is to be African-American.

Her studio is crowded with stuff!
She uses bows, feathers, and buttons
in her designs.

Sometimes, Ms. Moja uses African "Adinkra" cloth.

After the cloth is dyed, special designs are stamped on each piece.

Each stamp has an important meaning. Ms. Moja has new stamps and some that are very old.

Designing is only part of Ms. Moja's talent. Another part is picking just the right fabric and thread at the fabric store.

Ms. Moja also uses colorful fabrics from other countries. She enjoys traveling far away to find them!

She sews by hand and by machine.
Finally her creation is done.
It seems like magic, but it took
a lot of hard work.

Ms. Moja's clothes can be worn in different ways.

The sash of this costume can be
worn over the shoulder or
around the waist.

This beaded headdress was made in Asia. It is perfect for Ms. Moja to wear with one of her costumes.

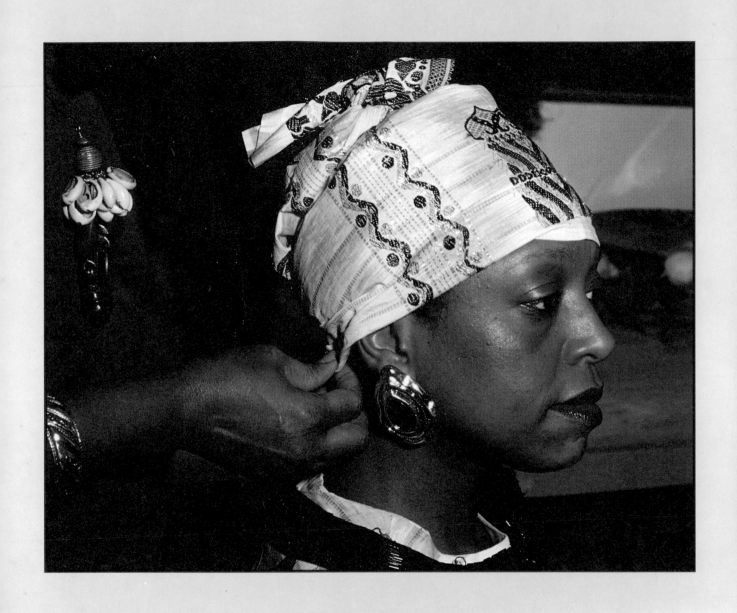

Headdresses are important for some of Ms. Moja's designs. She makes them out of cloth, beads, and feathers.

What a lovely coat Ms. Moja made!
It is a rainbow of yarn!

Ms. Moja started designing clothes when she was very young. Her grandmother taught her how to sew.

Ms. Moja makes very special clothes. This dress is like those worn by brides in some African countries.

Ms. Moja calls this costume "Starwoman."

She designed it to tell a story of how stars are born. Of all the costumes Ms. Moja has made, she loves this one the most.

Meet the Photographer
and the Author

Lili Duvall decided when she was in her teens that she wanted to take pictures. She is now a professional photographer and taking pictures of children is her favorite work. Her home and studio are in Maryland.

Jill Duvall, Lili's writing partner, is also her mother. Jill likes living near Washington, D.C., because much of her studying and writing is about the government. Jill feels that writing is very important and even takes her writing to the beach!